LITTLE
BY
LITTLE

TAJ ARORA

**THOUGHT
CATALOG**
Books

THOUGHTCATALOG.COM
NEW YORK · LOS ANGELES

THOUGHT CATALOG Books

Published by Thought Catalog Books, an imprint of the digital magazine Thought Catalog, which is owned and operated by The Thought & Expression Company LLC, an independent media organization based in Brooklyn, New York and Los Angeles, California.

This book was produced by Chris Lavergne and Noelle Beams with art direction and design by KJ Parish. Special thanks to Bianca Sparacino for creative editorial direction and Isidoros Karamitopoulos for circulation management.

Visit us at *thoughtcatalog.com* and *shop-catalog.com*.

Made in the United States.

ISBN 978-1-949759-34-1

You were a seed
hopeless and alone
in the darkness
unknowing of its own potential
to bloom

To know oneself means to unlearn
who you think you are
who you think you've been
and who you think you are becoming

I am just a vessel
for the message
trying to get to you

You'll know you've healed
when you find gratitude
in the pain
that once broke you

The knots in your chest
will dissolve
and you will learn
to breathe again

You were enough then and you are enough now
your pain never defined you, and never will

You've got to trust
that the light within you is enough
to guide you out of the darkness

Do not tell your friends to show up
as the wild women they are
while you hide yourself timidly in the shadows

It is not your job to fix people. I know your heart aches seeing the people you love in pain. But it is not your job to make their burden your own—that is not your path. You heal nobody by remaining stuck. It's only when you heal yourself that you show others the way out. *We heal by following the example of the healed.*

When you see beauty in another woman
it is you recognising the beauty within yourself

I do not fear the day I take my last breath
nor do I fear the loss of human life
I fear living each day suffocated in my own body
I fear never having explored the depths
of my own inner landscape
I fear never being able to untie myself
from the chains that hold me down
I fear never having the courage to
live out my wildest dreams
I do not fear death
I fear a life unlived

Telling women to cover up
is asking to put a veil
over God's creation
what is the point of art
if it can not be seen

The way you love
may look different
than the way
others love you

It doesn't mean
it's less

There is a world
more peaceful
than the one you're living in
the gateway is your breath

Your power lies within the courage to show
up as your truest, most authentic self

Our intuition has roots deep within the earth's core, we are one with it. Our hearts listen to the guidance of spirit without us even knowing. When you feel certain about a direction with no logical reason, it is ancient wisdom from your ancestors speaking to you. Listen to it. Always listen to it.

...but do you feel alive?

I know how desperately you wish for love. The kind of love that will hold your hand as you drift off to sleep. The kind of love that will make you laugh and cry until your belly hurts. The kind of love that isn't easy but worth it. The kind of love that hurts but only because you fear of losing it. The kind of love that will give you hope even on your darkest of days. Your heart craves a love that will complete you—a love that will make you see the world in a different way. But this love that you've been searching for was really always within you. You were never incomplete. Loving yourself is holding your own hand while you shake with anxiety. It's laughing at your own jokes, even the bad ones (*especially* the bad ones). Loving yourself is crying until your heart heals. It's sitting through pain for your own personal growth. You see, loving yourself isn't easy, but it will be worth it.

Anxiety is listening to your heartbeat
as you drift off to sleep
watching it fade away
wondering if this is how you die
then rising in the morning
and realising it has already passed
—*it will always pass*

My ancestors
did not bite their tongues
so I could live in silence

Do not become so obsessed with the direction of the arrow that you completely miss the mark. It doesn't matter how you get there, it's just that you do.

Wishing upon a dandelion
was always our way
of knowing that a higher power held us
we knew our dreams could come true

There is nothing wrong with an ordinary life
sometimes the biggest adventure is
within the little moments
that make up your normal day

Don't let your fear of doing it alone
stop you from doing it altogether

I do not wish for my children to grow up hating the vessel that has given them life. The body that lets them laugh, play, and cry. Your body is your home—a home you spend every second of your existence within. *There is nothing wrong with you.* There is nothing wrong with the way you look, and even if there were, it would not make you less worthy.

Imperfection is
the definition of beauty

Loss
is a funny thing
it confuses you
to believe
the ground beneath you
is shaking
when in fact
you're building
a whole new world

When you do decide to change
you might be misunderstood
by the people you have outgrown

But nothing else would make sense
to the people you are meant for

When we commit to our soul's deepest longing
and nurture our gift to the world
miracles happen
planets align
the whole universe conspires
to make our dreams come alive

You will not find happiness
outside of yourself
like the world tells you that you will
happiness is found within the depths of contentment
you feel for the life you have created

The colour of my skin
does not define my story

Self-love is not only loving the parts of yourself
you deem beautiful
but also the parts you'd rather hide away
knowing they are all
deserving

There is beauty within jealousy
because it shows you care
there is reflection within anger
clarity within fear
the envy and greed that runs through your veins
is the road map to your desires

As you shed your past
you become lighter
less burdened
and with that lightness
my love
you will fly

When you fully accept the dimples on your thighs and the tiger stripes that radiate from the centre of your chest, it becomes an empowering experience—not just for you but for all humans that were once told that they were anything but perfect.

When you can smile back at the woman in the mirror looking to you for hope, then you will know what it means to feel whole.

Wait for the storm to clear
and you might just be greeted
with the rainbow
you spent your life wishing for

Fear will teach you
what you care about most

In a world where we are constantly told self-love is the key, it's okay not to love yourself. There is no shame in looking for love within and not finding it. Not knowing how to love yourself doesn't make you unlovable. The doors will still open. You will find yourself in time. It is okay not to love yourself, and instead, just meet yourself where you stand.

Just because the world
requires you to be tough
doesn't mean
you can't be gentle with yourself

There is no going back
even on days
when the waves of pain
are most intense
remember you will never go back
there is only the future
there is only moving forward

What if our purpose
is just to know human life
as imperfectly as it is

It's okay to feel self-doubt from time to time
you chose to go beyond what you've known
and beyond what's kept you safe

So the next time you want to curl up in a ball
because you feel like you're not enough
remember this feeling is proof
that you chose not to stay small

I surrender to the universe
I trust the unfolding

When you silence your mind
and allow yourself to live
within the sensations of ecstasy
that exist within your body
you meet the edge
the portal between pain and pleasure

Some people are not ready to wake up
no matter how loudly you scream
honour their journey
they will listen when they are ready

One day
your future self
will thank you
for the chances
you took today

You can love the person you currently are
while working toward becoming someone better

In times of despair
reading became my saviour
the bond between each letter
was the strength that held me together

To change our outer worlds
we must look within
and if one finds nothing
but emptiness inside
then fill it with love
until it pours out of you

The mind is the doorway
to both heaven and hell

You will lose pieces of yourself
in the process of becoming and that's okay
those pieces were never meant for you to keep

Deconstruct the ego
and you'll be greeted
with a thirst for power
and an infatuation
with the past and future
and once that has subsided
you'll find resounding peace

How does one find love in a world
that values likes and shares over
deep human connection?

Don't you see
there are galaxies within you
waiting to be discovered

When you find the courage to love your own body, you give the people who look like you permission to do the same

I wonder how differently we would live if the world wasn't at our fingertips. Would we spend hours each day looking at screens or spend more time cooking with our families? Would we lose ourselves in a social media scroll or find ourselves through time spent alone? Would it matter what you wore or how much you weighed? Maybe if these distractions disappeared, we would discover that life's treasures were always buried in the present moment. The very moment that each notification tells us to run away from. I wonder how peacefully we would live if we didn't act as though life was in our phones.

Everything that hurts has
the potential to heal

The flower does not wait
for every seed in the field to sprout
before it begins to blossom

Why are you?

When you find peace within
solitude becomes sacred
an intimate moment
between time and spirit

Honour where you are right now

You discover your soul in the quiet moments you spend alone. You find yourself through your daily habits and routines, and by spending time with the ones that matter most. You find yourself by making peace with the thoughts that keep you up at night, by unlearning years of conditioning that teach you happiness can only be found in people, products, and places. The answers you are seeking are within you, it's society that's taught you to look outside of yourself.

Why is it that when we bleed
we are unholy
but without our unholiness
darling
you do not have life

The desire to heal oneself
is not selfish
it's the most selfless way
to serve the world

The enemy is not another woman's worth
it is a world that tells you that you
must compete for your own

Being vulnerable
is an act of courage
it requires you
to strip down
naked
with your heart on display

I hope you're brave enough
to let go of a future
that was never truly yours
that you never really wanted
that was imposed upon you
by dreams that were never
really your own

They tell us to love the heart of another but never to honour the very one beating within us. We spend more time dating others than learning to be content by ourselves. We dream about our weddings before our graduations. We search for our soulmates having never known our own souls.

Darling
you can stop holding your breath
your head is above water
—it always has been

Being heartbroken is a sign of strength
it shows you were brave enough
to love in the first place

You are your longest relationship
seduce yourself

Becoming is a sacred pilgrimage, a journey
back to the person you've always been

We live under the illusion
that tomorrow is guaranteed
every breath is a blessing
another opportunity to be

Losing yourself is realising
you were never the identity you had formed
you were something much deeper
and much greater

In times of uncertainty, may the moon be your grounding. The cycles are the same as those within you. No matter where you are, under its soft light, you are safe—knowing that even in the darkness, you are held.

The ones who don't want you to heal
are the ones who are getting something
from you being broken

True confidence comes from admitting that you are human—admitting that you make mistakes—and choosing to grow anyway.

Maybe when the world goes quiet
it's so that you can finally listen
to your heart's deepest longings

Whatever you do, please do not feel ashamed for who you once were. The decisions you made were primal instinct. The decisions you made were for survival. Your past self deserves your forgiveness and your gratitude.

Repeat this until you are breathless —
I promise to never give up on myself

You thought you were alone
until the words of a poet
reminded you
of our universal experience

We are all interconnected

You have to try even if right now it feels like your world is falling apart. There is great strength within that heart of yours. It knows how to move mountains. You see, growth doesn't come short of the growing pains—it's uncomfortable and messy. The burden you carry on your shoulders won't be there forever. I promise you're not always going to feel lost and alone. You have to try— only you can change your life.

·

May you always see the good in people
may you love as if you are immortal
may you practice kindness and gratitude
may you live a life that fulfills you

Maybe this time isn't about finding love but rather learning how to enjoy your own company instead. Maybe this time isn't about hustling for your dreams but rather slowing down and figuring out what's worth hustling for. Maybe the lesson is not how best to chase the things we think will make us happy but learning to be happy wherever we are instead.

Serendipity becomes a daily occurrence
when you step into who you were born to be

Asking for help is one of the
bravest things you can do

We were born to create. We have more than one purpose, one calling. Can you imagine a sky that would only be blue for the rest of eternity? Now wouldn't that be so boring? For the rain, the clouds, the thunder and storm is what gives the sky life. The freedom to shape shift—now that's what I call a living, breathing creation of God.

Never take advice from
anyone who dares not to live
out their own dreams

Saying no
only closes the wrong doors
and leads us to the right ones

Self-love is a prayer
a daily commitment to keep trying
no matter how much it hurts

With each passing year, I hope you don't fear growing old. I hope the day your knees fall weak and your hair turns grey is the same day your inner beauty shines with gratitude. I hope you see the stories the lines of wisdom across your face have told. Your grandchildren will learn to dream through you. You'll become a beacon of hope for the innocent minds that want to be told that life is beautiful, and that they, too, have the power to choose their own path. You see, beauty doesn't fade with age—it blossoms.

All we are really seeking is
a love that will listen

Life doesn't get easier
your foundations become stronger
even the tornado begins to feel like a gust of wind

Whatever you went through or are going through right now, you will heal from it. These wounds will turn into scars—scars you will bear with pride. The pain will one day be greeted with a smile. You'll feel immensely proud of your younger self for being so brave. Tears of joy will flow through you as you reflect on every lesson you learned through hardship and heartbreak. You'll see your pain became the catalyst for your growth.

Those who drain
the life force
from within you
are not your people

You have to understand that your existence is not a coincidence. You were put on this earth for a reason—you are meant to be here. Your life has meaning and purpose even if you don't know what that is yet.

Time only heals the wounds
we are willing to face

The smallest steps might seem like nothing
but you're moving forward
every day

Remember you are someone else's safe space
someone out there
looks to you
for hope
so maybe you could learn
to look to yourself

*Why do you keep working
when you deeply crave rest?*

Unknowingly, you will hurt people. Unknowingly, you will break hearts and disappoint and have to let go of what's not meant for you. Unknowingly, you will hurt people, and that's okay, because it will teach you that not all those who hurt you mean to.

Worrying is not keeping you safe
it's stealing your peace

When we express gratitude
for even the smallest of things
we tell the universe
we are ready for more

You're not meant to have your whole life figured out. These years are for trial and error—to see what works and what doesn't. It's not about making your parents proud. It's not about meeting every milestone the moment you think you should. Your life is meant for discovering how you want to live. It's about taking risks and making mistakes—failing and trying all over again. Your life is about forgiving all the things that went wrong and holding your head up high, knowing there are *always* better days ahead.

Resisting the current of the sea
will leave you exhausted
flow
and you might just end up
where you always wanted to be

Even hummingbirds are jealous
of the song your heart sings
when you're in love with what you do

I wish one day
to become fluent
in the language my body speaks
maybe then I'll understand
what it needs
to feel loved

Death is what makes
living so beautiful

The inner critic never goes away but you will learn to coexist with her. You will guide her with confidence through every challenge you encounter. You will comfort her when she's afraid. You will hear her tell you that you're crazy, that you're not enough, and you will have to correct her each time. You will feel her rise up in anxiety and you will learn to quiet her down. Your inner critic is here to stay, but you will learn to walk beside her.

Even the majestic oak tree
a symbol of strength
a connection between realms
needs years to grow
give yourself time

Find someone who doesn't try to tame your love
and embraces your wildness with open arms

I'm returning my limiting beliefs
back to their righteous owners

Loving yourself is not the same as being in love—self-love is not the same as romantic love. Loving yourself is honouring your boundaries and not tolerating disrespect. It's pushing past the fear that stands between you and your dreams. Loving yourself is having the courage to leave situations and people that are not serving your growth. Self-love is not something you feel, but rather something you do each day.

Take a deep breath
You are not your thoughts

Nothing is permanent,
not even your pain

There is no one in the history of the universe that has been created just like you

Who do you have to compete with?

The only thing that matters
is that in the end
you walked away
knowing you tried your best

If you want people to love you for who you are
then you need to love them for who they are
without expecting them to change

Pay close attention to the reason you get up in the morning. The daydreams you lose yourself in, the books that ignite your imagination, and the songs that make your atoms want to dance. Pay close attention to the people that energise you, the conversations that spark curiosity, and the jokes that make you laugh—these are the clues to your happiness.

Letting go
creates the space
we need to welcome
our wildest manifestations

Every time you don't set a boundary with someone else
you violate your own inner truth

Feeling lost is a sign
that you're finally listening to yourself
and no longer conforming
to what is expected of you

What if the very thing
you're avoiding
is what you need the most
rest my dear

rest

You will live many lifetimes
just within this one
many versions of you will exist
and each time you evolve
you will learn to shed your skin

How do you find clarity?

By asking yourself the questions you are afraid to ask, and then having the courage to listen to the answers that follow.

It was never about forgetting where you came from
it was about choosing to remember
so you could move on

A true soulmate would never dim your light
they only bring forth the sun within you

Whatever you do, please do not numb yourself. It is a gift to feel love, joy, sadness, anger, and fear. It is a gift to touch the surface of the ocean, the skin of another human being and the first warm sip of coffee that meets your lips every morning. Do not numb yourself with the illusionary chase we have been taught to believe is the meaning of life. Whatever you do, please do not numb yourself. Feel the heights of light and feel the depths of darkness. Dive deep into yourself and explore what's always been beneath. When you numb yourself from the pain that exists within your being, you numb yourself to the love that exists within the world.

Forgive all those who have been unkind to you
including yourself

Please do not doubt the good in your life. Do not let overthinking steal you of the joy you have been praying for. You deserve every ounce of success that exists in this world. The day you see the fruits of your labour, I hope you don't push it away. I hope you don't resist it by thinking you are unworthy. That couldn't be further from the truth. There are no moments that are too good to be true. You are worthy of everything you've set your mind to.

Art can exist
without explanation
so why must we understand
the complexities of life
to fully live it

We are children
of mother earth
thus with each new season
we ought to shed
like the coming of winter
and bloom like flowers
at the first sight of spring

Between what used to be
and what is yet to become
when the old ways
of thinking have dissolved
and the new perspectives
haven't formed
you will find yourself
in the middle of nowhere
but nowhere is still somewhere
trust that this too serves its purpose
there is something very magical
about the in-between

Be careful with the words
you whisper to yourself in silence
they have the power to make you weightless
or become the weight you carry for decades

The judgments that people have cast on you for how you do or do not appear is nothing more than just a projection of their own wounds—wounds that were sown generations ago, wounds that have yet to be healed. You don't have to take it personally. *It was never about you.*

Love is our greatest liberation

This moment right now
will one day become
a memory
feel it
in its entirety
before it's gone

One day you just stop caring. You stop caring about other people's accomplishments. You stop caring about the way they choose to live their lives. The gossip that used to excite you now bores you. It no longer frightens you that your friends are married and you're not. You would rather keep your head down and focus on your own dreams than compare yourself to how your peers are performing. One day you stop caring about what others think because what you think matters more.

And just like that
she became soft with every exhale

If you ever find yourself at crossroads, ask yourself this:

Which road brings me closer to peace and
which road takes me away from it?

Learn to see
through the eyes
of a child
they see magic
where we see mundane

You're not the same person you were a year ago
you've come farther than you remember

It is not your fault for falling in love with the wrong person. It is easy to mistake familiarity for love, if the love you received as a child was flawed. It is not your fault for confusing abuse as overprotection and violence with care—for seeking refuge in the wrong arms. It is not your fault for falling in love with what you thought was home.

I understand now
that every rose
must wilt before
it can be reborn

If your ribcage expands
at the thought
that something out there
is waiting for you
then you must go
and not rest until you find it

TAJ ARORA is a transformational life coach, writer, and photographer from London.

tajarora.com
instagram.com/tajaroraa

THOUGHT CATALOG Books

Thought Catalog Books is a publishing imprint of Thought Catalog, a digital magazine for thoughtful storytelling. Thought Catalog is owned by The Thought & Expression Company, an independent media group based in Brooklyn, NY, which also owns and operates Shop Catalog, a curated shopping experience featuring our best-selling books and one-of-a-kind products, and Collective World, a global creative community network. Founded in 2010, we are committed to helping people become better communicators and listeners to engender a more exciting, attentive, and imaginative world. As a publisher and media platform, we help creatives all over the world realize their artistic vision and share it in print and digital form with audiences across the globe.

ThoughtCatalog.com | **Thoughtful Storytelling**

ShopCatalog.com | **Boutique Books + Curated Products**

Collective.world | **Creative Community Network**

**MORE FROM
THOUGHT CATALOG BOOKS**

The Strength In Our Scars
—Bianca Sparacino

The Mountain Is You
—Brianna Wiest

Everything You'll Ever Need
(You Can Find Within Yourself)
—Charlotte Freeman

Your Heart Is The Sea
—Nikita Gill

**THOUGHT
CATALOG**
Books

THOUGHTCATALOG.COM
NEW YORK · LOS ANGELES